Mother Teresa

By Susan Eddy

Consultant
Jeanne Clidas, Ph.D.
National Reading Consultant
and
Professor of Reading, SUNY Brockport

Children's Press ®
A Division of Scholastic Inc.
New York Toronto London Auckland Sydney
Mexico City New Delhi Hong Kong
Danbury, Connecticut

Designer: Herman Adler Design
Photo Researcher: Caroline Anderson
The photo on the cover shows Mother Teresa.

Library of Congress Cataloging-in-Publication Data

Eddy, Susan.
  Mother Teresa / by Susan Eddy ; consultant, Jeanne Clidas.
     p. cm. – (Rookie biographies)
Includes index.
Summary: A brief overview of the life of Mother Teresa who dedicated her
life to helping the poor in India and was awarded the Nobel Peace Prize
for her work.
  ISBN 0-516-25881-8 (lib. bdg.)   0-516-27922-X (pbk.)
  1. Teresa, Mother, 1910—Juvenile literature. 2. Missionaries of
Charity–Biography–Juvenile literature. [1. Teresa, Mother, 1910-
2. Missionaries. 3. Nobel prizes–Biography. 4. Women–Biography.]
I. Clidas, Jeanne. II. Title. III. Series: Rookie biography.
  BX4406.5.Z8E33 2003
  271'.97–dc21

                            2003004589

©2003 by Scholastic Inc.
All rights reserved. Published simultaneously in Canada.
Printed in China.

CHILDREN'S PRESS, and ROOKIE BIOGRAPHIES™, and associated
logos are trademarks and or registered trademarks of Scholastic Library
Publishing. SCHOLASTIC and associated logos are trademarks and or
registered trademarks of Scholastic Inc.
7 8 9 10 11 12 13 14 15 R 12 11 10   62

Mother Teresa made the
world a better place.

She did the work that no one else wanted to do. She helped poor people.

Her name was not always Teresa.
Agnes Gonxha Bojaxhiu (AG-nes
GOHN-jah BOY-yah-jee-oo)
was born in Macedonia on
August 26, 1910.

When she was 12 years old, she heard a missionary (MISH-uh-ner-ee) speak about the homeless in India.

A missionary is someone who travels to another country to help people.

A missionary helping children

9

Saint Teresa

Six years later, Agnes decided to become a nun. She named herself "Teresa" after a saint she admired.

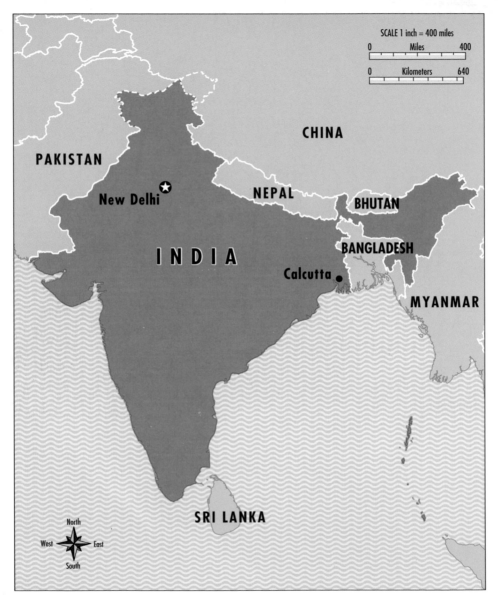

She was a teacher in Calcutta
for 17 years. Her students
loved her.

Her school was beautiful, but Sister Teresa was not happy.

People were living in slums. Slums are crowded and poor areas of a city or town.

Sister Teresa wanted to help these people.

Sister Teresa left the school to work in the slums. She took off her nun's habit and put on a white cotton sari (SAH-ree).

A sari is a long piece of cloth
that is used for clothing. The
sari cost one dollar. It was what
poor people wore.

She traveled to another city to learn about sickness and medicine.

Then, she went back to Calcutta. She began to help the children.

19

Sister Teresa fed the children.
She taught them to wash.
She taught them the alphabet
(AL-fuh-bet). She taught them
about love.

They called her Mother Teresa.

One day, Mother Teresa carried a sick woman to a hospital. They were turned away. The hospital had too many patients.

So, Mother Teresa started a special place for poor people who were sick.

Mother Teresa and her helpers
carried sick people off the streets.

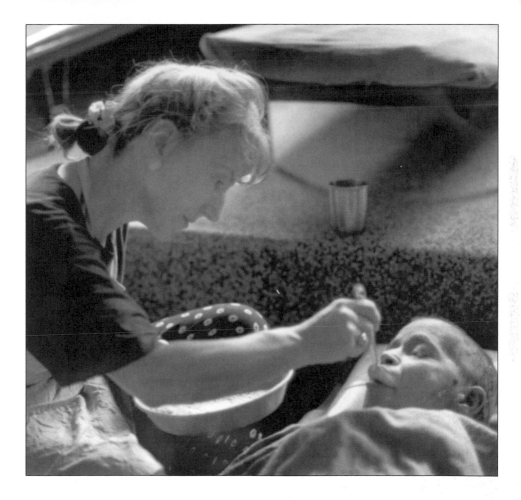

They washed them and made
them comfortable.

Mother Teresa won the Nobel Peace Prize in 1979. She wore her cotton sari to receive the world's greatest honor.

Mother Teresa died peacefully in 1997.

Today, 4,500 nuns in 120 countries carry on her work. They do little things with great love.

Words You Know

India

Macedonia

missionary

Mother Teresa

30

nuns

Nobel Peace Prize

sari

slums

31

Index

About the Author

Susan Eddy grew up in New Jersey but has loved New York City all her life. She is an editor by profession and an avocational singer who especially enjoys writing nonfiction books for children. These days she divides her time between a small farm in New Jersey and a small brownstone in Greenwich Village.

Photo Credits

Photographs © 2003: AP/Wide World Photos: cover (Chris Bacon), 26, 31 top right (Henrik Laurvik), 24; Corbis Images: 20; Dinodia Picture Agency/Swnil K. Dutt: 5, 17; Hulton|Archive/Getty Images: 9, 13, 30 bottom left; Magnum Photos/Bruno Barbey: 15, 31 bottom right; Sovfoto/Eastfoto: 29, 31 top left (Igor Zehl), 6; The Image Works: 3, 30 bottom right (Louise Gubb), 25 (Sean Sprague), 16, 31 bottom left (Topham); TRIP Photo Library: 10, 19 (H Rogers), 23 (J Sweeney).

Maps by Bob Italiano